21 Days of Growth

Hetanshi Joshi

BookLeaf Publishing

Presentation by *BookLeaf Publishing*

Web: www.bookleafpub.com

E-mail: info@bookleafpub.com

ISBN: 9789357441438

First edition 2023

This book is dedicated to my loved ones.

Child's dream

Once upon a time, there was a small child
Who had a dream of running wild
The child ran far, far away
To explore a world full of play

The sun was bright and the birds sang
The child laughed and danced and sang
The child ran through the meadows and streams
And imagined a life of many dreams

The child ran until the night
Then stopped to gaze at the starry sky
The child thought of all the possibilities
Of a life that would be full of bliss

The child let out a happy sigh
And knew that no matter what, they'd try
To make that dream their reality
And leave the world with a lasting legacy

Beautiful nature

The sky is so blue, the birds sing a tune
The trees are so tall, with leaves of them all

The sun is so bright, it warms us all day
The clouds in the sky, roll away

The grass is so green, the flowers so bright
The wind is so cool, it feels just right

The lake is so calm, like a mirror in the sky
The sky is a reminder, of the beauty all around

It's nature we can see, on the ground and in the
sky
It's nature that we can touch, with its beauty that
never dies

It's nature that brings us joy, and gives us peace
of mind
It's nature that's so divine, it's hard to leave
behind.

Wakeup call

3

Reality is a funny thing,
It can change the way we sing.

It can make us feel so small,
Or it can lift us up and make us tall.

It can bring a world of joy,
Filling our hearts with purest joy.

It can also bring us pain,
And make us cry in the rain.

Reality can be harsh and cruel,
But it can also be so cool.

It can be an adventure,
A journey that's worth the venture.

Reality is what we make it,
No matter how hard we fake it.

It's our truth, our story,
Our reality, our glory.

Life, Existence, Death

Life is a fleeting dream,
In which we all seek to glean,
A precious knowledge of our fate,
To help us navigate.

Existence is a mystery,
A winding path with no history,
We stumble through the darkness blind,
Each step a risk of what we'll find.

Death is a final destination,
Separating our joys and elation,
From the troubles and worries of life,
Towards a future without strife.

Long night

The night is dark, my thoughts alight
A raging storm within my mind
My heart is heavy, my soul in flight
Depression has me firmly pinned

I'm caught in an endless cycle of doubt
My mind is spinning, I can't get out
My thoughts, they spiral, I can't control
The fear, the worry, my aching soul

My thoughts, they cloud and take me down
The fear of failure weighs me down
The depression deepens, I can't escape
The darkness grips, I'm in its grasp

I need to be free, I need a way out
I need to find peace, to no longer doubt
I need to believe in myself, it's time to fight
I need to be brave and shine my light

The darkness will pass and I will be free
The overthinking will cease and I will be me
My courage will guide me through the night
I will be strong and I will be alright

Forgive and Forget

Betrayal and jealousy can cause such pain,
When trust is shattered it can drive you insane.

Friends can be like family, a bond deep and true,
But the slightest of cracks can cause the whole
thing to undo.

Jealousy can consume, with its dark and twisted
lies,
The feelings of betrayal are like a stab to the
eyes.

But even through all the pain and the broken
trust,
A friend will be with you no matter how long or
a must.

No matter how dark the clouds may seem,
Your friends will be there to help you dream.

Dark and Light

The night is dark, my thoughts alight
A raging storm within my mind
My heart is heavy, my soul in flight
Depression has me firmly pinned

I'm caught in an endless cycle of doubt
My mind is spinning, I can't get out
My thoughts, they spiral, I can't control
The fear, the worry, my aching soul

My thoughts, they cloud and take me down
The fear of failure weighs me down
The depression deepens, I can't escape
The darkness grips, I'm in its grasp

I need to be free, I need a way out
I need to find peace, to no longer doubt
I need to believe in myself, it's time to fight
I need to be brave and shine my light

The darkness will pass and I will be free
The overthinking will cease and I will be me
My courage will guide me through the night
I will be strong and I will be alright

love

A boy and a girl had a love that was true
Their hearts beat as one, in a blissful hue

The stars shone so bright, their love was a light
The two were enthralled, in each other's sight

The boy was so gentle, his touch was divine
The girl was so beautiful, she made him so fine

Their love was a wonder, like a rose in bloom
The two of them together, was a special kind of zoom

The boy and the girl, made a promise that day
That their love would be strong, as it flew on its way

So hand in hand, they walked to the shore
Where they will remain, forever more

what a girl thinks.

A timid, shy girl, so full of care
Too afraid to speak her mind, she wouldn't dare
Her emotions she does always share
Her heart, she has laid out there

When she's upset, she'll never shout
But rather, quietly, she'll pout
For she fears to rock the boat
And she'd rather not take the vote

She's a people pleaser, it's true
So she'll always put others before her view
But when she reaches the breaking point
She'll gather courage and make her own joint

She's not afraid to take a stand
For her own beliefs, she'll demand
Though the road is long and hard
Still, she'll cling to her guard

A timid, shy girl, full of care
May she have the strength to always dare.

A second chance

A second chance is like a bright light
That shines in the night
It gives us the hope to forgive
And look past a person's misdeeds

We can all make mistakes
And it's ok to take the time to learn
Forgiveness can be a hard thing
But it's worth the work in the end

So don't be afraid to give a second chance
And accept that people grow and change
It's not easy to forgive and forget
But it's the right thing to do to arrange

Start with a kind word and an open heart
And try to put yourself in someone else's shoes
It's possible to find understanding and peace
When you forgive, you can be free to choose

new life

The world is wide and life is grand,
A new city is where I'll stand.
Though I'm feeling a bit of fear,
It's a new adventure that I'll revere.

This journey will have its highs and lows,
But I'm ready to face whatever it throws.
The people I'll meet and the places I'll go,
Are all part of the journey, I'm sure I know.

I'll explore the city, try new things,
Dive deep into all life brings.
The new people I'll meet and the old I'll stay in
touch,
Will help me to make this new city feel like
home so much.

So here I am, ready to start,
This new life in this new place with an open
heart.
I'm ready to grow and learn and love,
In this new city that I'm thinking of.

long lost cousins

Two strangers in a café,
One from near, the other far.
Fate brought them both together,
But their connection was never clear.

One was from the city,
The other from the country side.
One was young and outgoing,
The other had a more reserved pride.

The two talked and laughed and shared,
Though they felt no relation at all.
But little did they know they were cousins,
With a bond that was deep and tall.

Though they were two strangers in a café,
They formed a familial connection.
The bond of a family was found,
From a random and unexpected selection.

old people

An old couple in love,
Their hearts still beat as one,
A bond of love so strong,
That it will never be undone.

Through years of joy and pain,
Through laughter and through tears,
Their love has only grown,
Through the passing of the years.

No matter what life throws,
No matter what they'll face,
The love they share will never end,
It's a bond they can't replace.

Their story's written in the stars,
A tale of tenderness and care,
An old couple in love,
A love that's always there.

Balance

Attachment comes in many forms,
It can bring both negative and positive norms.

We can become attached to material things,
Which can cause fear and sadness it brings.

We can become attached to people too,
But sometimes with them, it's not what we knew.

We can become attached to our hopes and
dreams,
Which can cause us to become stuck it seems.

Positivity and negativity need to exist,
Balance is needed for our mental health to
persist.

Both emotions have their place in life,
So, we must find our inner strife.

When we can find joy and peace within,
We can find the balance of attachment and
begin.

brave and courageous

She stands tall and proud, her spirit soaring high
A force of nature, whose beauty never dies
Her strength and courage, like a beacon in the
night
Her voice is her power, her courage her might

She knows what she wants, and will never back
down
That strong will of hers, will never be found
She'll stand up for herself, and for all other
women too
For feminism and woman empowerment, she
will never be through

She's determined and brave, she's a warrior at
heart
A fighter of justice, no matter what the cost
She can do anything, and she won't be denied
For in her heart and soul, she knows the truth of
her pride

A champion of the cause, she's a source of light
Her will and strength, a powerful might
For all the women she loves and for all those
who stand strong
She'll never stop fighting, she'll lead us along

white life

Racism, a plague of our society,
That makes us so blind to our diversity.
It's a horrid thing, that's so hard to explain,
That we judge people based on their skin and
their name.

It's humanity that we must embrace,
And remember that we all share space.
No matter our color, our language, our creed,
We are all connected in this life that we lead.

Let's come together and eradicate this bane,
And learn to accept, love and sustain.
Let's not be divided and create more strife,
But stand together and create a better life.

Let's open our minds, to all different kinds,
And judge not a person, by their gender or skin.
For all of us have value, from history and from
faith,
And it's up to us to end this hate.

strong words

Stand up and speak out against the abuse
End the cycle of violence and the misuse
Gender-based violence is no excuse
Awareness must be raised, we must refuse

We must not let fear be our undoing
A safe and equal world is our pursuit of
something
It's time to stand up, we can't remain silent
For true equality, we must be defiant

Empowerment is key to our success
Equality should not just be a guess
Men, women, people of all ages
Must understand and turn the pages

We must come together, all hands must join
For a world free of abuse, a common goal to
coin
We must take a proactive stance
And not let fear or silence take us to chance

The future is in our hands
A world free from violence, a new chance
We must stand together, no matter our gender
And strive for an equal world, now and forever.

Faith and Hope

The moon, the sun, and the stars,
It's a beautiful sight, near and far.
It brings us joy and peace of mind,
The beauty that can be hard to find.

The night sky twinkles and shines,
A blanket of stars so divine.
The moon glows brightly up above,
Bringing us all hope and love.

The morning sun brings a new day,
A chance to start fresh and make our way.
It's a reminder of life and light,
Everything is alright.

The stars sparkle and fill the night,
The night sky is a glorious sight.
It's a reminder of faith and hope,
And that even in darkness, we can cope.

The moon, the sun, and the stars,
It's a beautiful sight, near and far.
It brings us joy and peace of mind,
The beauty that can be hard to find.

Time is money

Time is precious, do not waste it,
For time does not wait for anyone.
It's a gift that can be taken away,
So don't waste a single day.

Time is a gift that should be spent,
For that's what life's about, content.
We all have days that we can't control,
But use the time that you have, whole.

Time can't be bought, no matter the price,
So, use it wisely, and not think twice.
A day wasted can never be regained,
So, make sure you use it, and never complain.

Time is precious, it's a valuable thing,
So, use it well, and don't forget to sing.
It's a unique journey, each day and night,
So, use it wisely, and make it right.